Natasha Alexandrova

Workbook 2

Russian Step By Step

for Children

Editors: Ellen Weaver, Anna Watt

Illustrations: Elena Litnevskaya

Cover: Natalia Illarionova

russianstepbystepforchildren.com

First Edition

Russian Step By Step for Children Workbook   2

All rights reserved

Copyright © 2016 by Russian Step By Step

ISBN-13:   978-1537287355

ISBN-10:   1537287354

Printed in the United States of America

Наташа Александрова

Книга студента 2

Русский шаг за шагом

для детей

Редакторы: Елена Вивер, Анна Вотт

Иллюстрации Елены Литневской

Обложка Натальи Илларионовой

russianstepbystepforchildren.com

4

Contents

Course Components

Welcome to the Russian Step By Step Learning System!

Russian Step By Step Workbook 2 is the second step in this series.

This course includes a ***Workbook*** and the corresponding ***Audio*** (Direct Download from our website).

We recommend that you listen to all the audio tracks, even if some of the exercises were covered in class. Please listen to the past lessons, as that helps with retention. Listen to the audio in the car, while walking, working out, cooking – the more you can incorporate the audio tracks into your everyday activities, the more you will improve your *retention, comprehension, and pronunciation.*

FREE Audio Component

By purchasing this book, you receive the **FREE audio** component right away!

To access the complimentary **Direct Digital Audio Download** please:

➢ Go to RussianStepByStepChildren.com/Registration   Make sure you are on the correct website, as there is a Russian Step By Step Series for Adults (It has a different website).

➢ Create your username and password

➢ After registration you will receive an email to verify your email address. Press the verification link, and **you are ready to listen!**

➢ Download the audio tracks on your computer through the top menu: Books > RSBS for Children > Audio Download

➢ If you have any questions, please email us at info@russianstepbystep.com

Structure of the Workbook 2

The *Workbook* has five parts: Primary Course, Grammar, Audio Script, Answer Key, and Dictionaries.

The ***Primary Course*** section consists of 6 lessons. Each lesson introduces new words and new grammar that are practiced in the exercises.

The ***Grammar*** section corresponds to the 6 lessons in the Primary Course. Here you will find explanations of new language and grammar rules that will help you use this language properly. In this section you will also find translations of new vocabulary.

The ***Audio Script*** section has the script which corresponds to the audio recorded by native speakers and will help you to improve your Russian pronunciation and fluency.

The ***Answer Key*** section provides the answers to the exercises.

The ***Dictionaries***: Adjectives are given in their masculine form. Words are given with the definitions that are used in this book.

Dear Adults!

Our Series *Russian Step By Step for Children* consists of many steps. Every book is another step that brings engaging and successful lessons of the Russian Language to the children.

This Series is designed for children in elementary and middle school (8 - 14 years old).

For children in preschool and kindergarten – please use our series *Azbuka*.

For children in high school, college students and adults – please use our series *Russian Step By Step School Edition.*

This series is a step-by-step introduction to the Russian language for children who do not speak Russian or have a limited exposure to the Russian language. Depending on the level of the child, you can begin using any step of this series.

Our series consists of a *Workbook*, *Audio* (Direct Download for a website), a *Teacher's Manual, Slides, and Games*. If you are a parent or a relative of the child and will be leading the lessons, you will require the *Teacher's Manual*. If you are a teacher - we promise that the *Teacher's Manual* will greatly facilitate your lesson plan preparation and significantly cut your lesson prep time.

Upon completion of this book you will learn some spelling rules, adjective declensions in gender, polite and informal greetings, colors, counting 11 – 20, talking about family, first name, patronymic, last name, formal and informal names.

For the Parents and Relatives of the Children Who Will use the Book

Please read the instructions on how to work with this book. You will be the biggest helper to the child outside of the classroom, even if you do not know any Russian.

1. At the end of the book you will find grammar explanations and translations. You do not have to cover them, but if the child expresses interest or asks you about some details they talked in class, this part will help you give the correct answers.

2. Use the audio at home not only as part of the homework assignments, but also to cement the covered material. Listen not only to the last lesson, but to at least three preceding lessons. This will help you to memorize the previously covered material.

3. The Workbook contains a certain specifically selected amount of material that the student needs. The main outline of the lesson is located in the Teacher's Manual. If you use this to study by yourself, please start from the Teacher's Manual.

4. Cover all the exercises in the lesson first orally and then in writing. It would be good to assign the exercises as written homework, after you have covered them orally in class. This repeated use helps to reinforce the new material.

5. The guiding principle of this book is that the children do not need to be presented with a large volume of new information (grammar, vocabulary). It is more important to work and play with the material presented in each lesson, until the student feels comfortable with it. So do not rush – high speed of

presentation and a large volume of new material only make the lesson harder for the children. If you want to add something to the lesson – use the additional components of this series (games, handouts, slides) that cover the same vocabulary and grammar.

Primary Course

Русский алфавит

А а   *Аа*   Б б   *Бб*   В в   *Вв*   Г г   *Гг*

Д д   *Дд*   Е е   *Ее*   Ё ё   *Ёё*   Ж ж   *Жж*

З з   *Зз*   И и   *Ии*   Й й   *Йй*   К к   *Кк*

Л л   *Лл*   М м   *Мм*   Н н   *Нн*   О о   *Оо*

П п   *Пп*   Р р   *Рр*   С с   *Сс*   Т т   *Тт*

У у   *Уу*   Ф ф   *Фф*   Х х   *Хх*   Ц ц   *Цц*

Ч ч   *Чч*   Ш ш   *Шш*   Щ щ   *Щщ*   ъ   *ъ*

ы   *ы*   ь   *ь*   Э э   *Ээ*   Ю ю   *Юю*

Я я   *Яя*

Урок 1

Pairs of Vowels: А - Я

А ⟶ **Я** [йа]

1

Упражнение 1

Listen to the audio and repeat syllables with hard and soft vowels after the native speaker.

ба – бя; ла – ля; да – дя; на – ня; са – ся; ра – ря;

мяч

няня

гиря

тётя Ира

дядя Коля

ряд

Упражнение 2

Listen to the words with hard and soft vowels and repeat after the native speaker.

1. Банк – бя́ка;   2. Лари́са – Ля́ля;   3. брат – ряд;   4. Са́ша – Ва́ся;   5. Нина – няня;

6. матч – мяч;   7. дама – дядя;   8. такси - тётя;   9. опера – гиря;   10. Шура – Боря.

Formal and Informal Names

Formal Name	Informal Name
Мари́я	Ма́ша
Ива́н	Ва́ня
Ната́лья	Ната́ша
Алекса́ндр	Са́ша
А́нна	А́ня
Па́вел	Па́ша
О́льга	О́ля
Да́рья	Да́ша
Степа́н	Стёпа
Серге́й	Серёжа
Светла́на	Све́та
Ви́ктор	Ви́тя
Денис	Дениска
Мари́на	Мари́ша

Упражнение 3

Russian names can be tricky for a foreigner, as the formal names differ from the corresponding informal names. Put the following names into the correct column.

Стёпа, Наташа, Ваня, Лара, Миша, Володя, Саша, Коля, Оля, Даша, Лёша, Маша, Ниночка, Рита, Петя, Саша, Витя, Боря, Света, Мариша.

Boy's Formal	Boy's Informal	Girl's Formal	Girl's Informal
Степан	**Стёпа**	Дарья	
Иван		Мария	
Пётр		Марина	
Виктор		Александра	
Борис		Лариса	
Александр		Нина	
Михаил		Наталья	
Николай		Ольга	
Владимир		Светлана	
Алексей		Маргарита	

And now please work with audio **Track 3**.

Здравствуй или здравствуйте?

Здравствуй, Оля.

Привет, Оля.

Здравствуйте, Светлана.

 Упражнение 4

Greet the following people.

1.  Рита ___**Здравствуй, Рита.**_____

2. Мария _____

3. Виктор _____

4. Иван _____

5. доктор _____

6. бабушка _____

Как вас зовут?

Здравствуйте, я Иван. Ты Оля. Вы Светлана. Мы Антон и Нина.

Меня зовут Иван. Тебя зовут Оля. Вас зовут Светлана. Нас зовут Антон и Нина.

Я	ТЫ	ВЫ	МЫ
меня	тебя	вас	нас

Упражнение 5

Create questions and answer them, following the example.

Образец: 1. Как тебя зовут?

Тебя зовут Саша.

1. Ты Саша. 2. Вы Ирина. 3. Я Антон. 4. Мы Нина и Зина. 5. Я Маргарита.

6. Вы Линда. 7. Ты Том. 8. Ты Моника. 9. Мы Маша и Даша. 10. Ты Аня.

And now please work with audio **Track 3**.

Урок 2

Pairs of Vowels: Э - Е

Э ⟶ Е [йе]

Упражнение 6

 4

Listen to the audio and repeat syllables with hard and soft vowels after the native speaker.

мэ – ме; лэ – ле; тэ – те; нэ – не; сэ – се; рэ – ре.

Упражнение 7

 5

Listen to the words with hard and soft vowels and repeat after the native speaker.

1. Меня́; 2. тебя́; 3. Мэ́ри; 4. телефо́н; 5. пробле́ма; 6. Дэ́вид; 7. галере́я;
8. интерне́т; 9. инжене́р; 10. балери́на; 11. карате́; 12. моме́нт.

Какой/какая?

- Кто это?
- Это де́вочка.
- Кака́я это девочка?
- Это у́мная девочка.

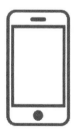

- Что это?
- Это телефон.
- Какой это телефон?
- Это хороший телефон.

Adjectives

он	она
Как**о́й**?	Как**а́я**?
хоро́ш**ий**	хоро́ш**ая**
у́мн**ый**	у́мн**ая**

Упражнение 8

Create pairs of questions and answers with the following words, using an adjective **хоро́ший**.

1. ла́мпа **Какая это лампа? Это хорошая лампа.**

2. рестора́н _____

3. кни́га _____

4. галере́я _____

5. парк _____

6. балери́на _____

7. шокола́д _____

8. мяч _____

9. спортсме́нка _____

10. ма́льчик _____

11. ёлка _____

And now please work with audio **Track 6**.

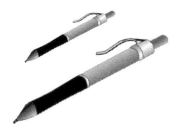

Это ру́чка. Она больша́я.

То тоже ручка. Она ма́ленькая.

Это цветок. Он краси́вый.

Это снежи́нка. Она холо́дная.

Это ма́льчик. Он весёлый.

Упражне́ние 9

Write down pairs of sentences, using a noun and an adjective.

1. сок/холодны́й ___**Это сок. Он холодный**_____

2. А́нна/краси́вый _____

3. президе́нт/у́мный _____

4. рестора́н/хоро́ший _____

5. ба́бушка/до́брый _____

6. стол/большо́й _____

7. ка́ска/ма́ленький _____

8. соба́ка/у́мный _____

9. журна́л/интере́сный _____

And now please work with audio **Track** 7.

Посчитаем! 11 - 20

11 – оди́ннадцать;

12 – двена́дцать;

13 – трина́дцать;

14 – четы́рнадцать;

15 – пятна́дцать;

16 – шестна́дцать;

17 – семна́дцать;

18 – восемна́дцать;

19 – девятна́дцать;

20 – два́дцать.

 ## Упражнение 10

Match the numbers and the words.

пять   **13**   три   **15**   двадцать   **11**

семнадцать   **3**   тринадцать   **6**

восемнадцать   **19**   ноль   один

0   шесть   **4**   двенадцать   двадцать   **1**

20   одиннадцать   **17**   пятнадцать   **18**

четыре   **5**   девятнадцать   **12**

And now please work with audio **Track** 8.

Урок 3

Pairs of Vowels: О - Ё

О ⟶ Ё [йо]

Упражнение 11

 9

Listen to the audio and repeat syllables with hard and soft vowels after the native speaker.

во – вё; мо – мё; ло – лё; то – тё; но – нё; со – сё; ро – рё.

Упражнение 12

 10

Listen to the words with hard and soft vowels and repeat after the native speaker.

1. Антон – Стёпа;   2. Лóра – Лёша;   3. Том – тётя;   4. сок – весёлый;   5. Боря – ребёнок; 6. Зоя – козёл;   7. мост – мёд;   6. нос;   8. самолёт;   9. актёр.

ребёнок   актёр   нос

мёд   козёл

Какой/какая/какое?

он	она	оно
Как**о́й**?	Как**а́я**?	Как**о́е**?
больш**о́й**	больш**а́я**	больш**о́е**
у́мн**ый**	**у́**мн**ая**	**у́**мн**ое**
ма́леньк**ий**	**ма́**леньк**ая**	**ма́**леньк**ое**

Телефо́н чёрный.

Бума́га бе́лая.

Со́лнце жёлтое.

Я́блоко кра́сное.

Мо́ре си́нее.

Цвет

Color the cells of the table accordingly.

бе́лый цвет	чёрный цвет	кра́сный цвет	жёлтый цвет	зелёный цвет	си́ний цвет

And now please work with audio **Track 11**.

 # Упражнение 13

Answer the following questions, as in the example.

1. Бана́н си́ний? (жёлтый) _____**Нет, банан не синий. Банан жёлтый.**_____

   _____

2. Мо́ре кра́сное? (синий) _____

   _____

3. Ла́мпа чёрная? (белый) _____

   _____

4. Авока́до белое? (зелёный) _____

   _____

5. Ру́чка зелёная? (чёрный) _____

   _____

6. Бума́га кра́сная? (синий) _____

   _____

7. Крокоди́л бе́лый? (зелёный) _____

   _____

Какого цвета?

- Что это?
- Это клубни́ка.
- Како́го она цве́та?
- Она кра́сная.

- Что это тако́е?
- Это огуре́ц.
- Како́го цве́та огуре́ц?
- Огуре́ц зелёный.

And now please work with audio **Track 12**.

 Упражнение 14

Ask questions and answer them using the following pairs of words.

1. со́лнце/жёлтый _____**Како́го цвета солнце? Оно жёлтое.**_____

2. компью́тер/чёрный _____

3. такси́/си́ний _____

4. меню́/бе́лый _____

5. огуре́ц/зелёный _____

6. ро́за/кра́сный _____

7. ли́лия/ синий _____

8. молоко́/белый _____

9. борщ/кра́сный _____

10. ёлка/ зелёный _____

11. сви́тер/си́ний _____

12. лимо́н/жёлтый _____

And now please work with audio **Track 13**.

Упражнение 15

Practice writing Russian numbers.

11   **одиннадцать**   12 _____

13 _____   14 _____

15 _____   16 _____

17 _____   18 _____

19 _____   20 _____

Урок 4

Pairs of Vowels: У - Ю

У ⟶ Ю [йу]

14

Упражнение 16

Listen to the audio and repeat syllables with hard and soft vowels after the native speaker.

му – мю; лу – лю; ту – тю; ну – ню; су – сю; ру – рю.

Упражнение 17

15

Listen to the words with hard and soft vowels and repeat after the native speaker.

1. мýзыка – мю́сли; 2. спýтник – пюрé; 3. лук – люк; 4. турúст – костю́м;

5. рýчка – брю́ки; 6. Людмúла; 7. студéнт; 8. Тимýр.

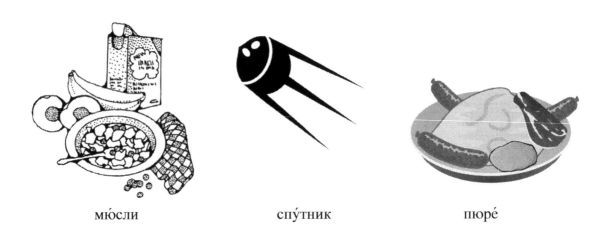

мю́сли   спýтник   пюрé

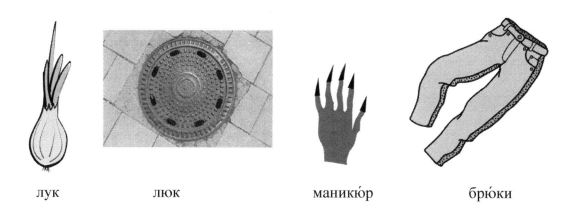

лук   люк   маникю́р   брю́ки

Справа – слева

Где пету́х? Он вот здесь сле́ва.   А где змея́? Она вот здесь спра́ва.

Упражнение 18

Look at the picture on the next page and answer questions, as in the example.

Образец: Он вот здесь справа.

1. Где жира́ф?   2. Где жук?   3. Где слон?   4. Где щено́к?   5. Где конь?   6. Где тигр?   7. Где кот?   8. Где змея́?   9. Где ёж?   10. Где панте́ра?   11. Где пчела́? 12. Где крокоди́л? 13. Где зебра́?

- Какого цвета слон?

- Он се́рый.

- Кто ещё серый?

– Ёж. Ёж тоже серый.

Его, её, их

Она Рита.

Её зовут Рита.

Он Дмитрий.

Его зовут Дмитрий.

Они Саша и Паша.

Их зовут Саша и Паша.

	(я)	меня́		Меня́ зову́т Джеймс.
	(ты)	тебя́		Тебя́ зову́т О́ля.
	(он)	его́		Его́ зову́т Оле́г.
Как	(она)	её	зову́т?	Её зову́т Та́ня.
	(вы)	вас		Вас зову́т Никола́й Петро́вич.
	(мы)	нас		Нас зову́т Ольга и Рау́ль.
	(они)	их		Их зову́т Еле́на и Серге́й.

Упражнение 19

Create questions and answer them, following the example.

Образец: 1. Как его зовут?
Его зовут Паша.

1. Он Па́ша. 2. Она Мари́на. 3. Я Маргари́та. 4. Они Зо́я и И́ра. 5. Мы Ольга и Дмитрий. 6. Вы Наташа. 7. Ты Джон. 8. Он Джеймс. 9. Она На́стя. 10. Он Степа́н. 11. Она Тама́ра. 12. Они Никола́й и Виктор.

Сколько будет?

$$1 \quad + \quad 3 \quad = \quad 4$$

Оди́н плюс три бу́дет четы́ре.

$$7 \quad - \quad 5 \quad = \quad 2$$

Семь ми́нус пять бу́дет два.

 ## Упражнение 20

Please calculate and write down answers, following the example.

1) 6 + 2 = __**Шесть плюс два будет восемь.**__

2) 7 − 1 = _____

3) 10 − 5 = _____

4) 9 + 9 = _____

5) 16 − 2 = _____

6) 17 − 1 = _____

7) $20 - 5 =$ _____

8) $8 + 1 =$ _____

9) $19 - 1 =$ _____

And now please work with audio **Track 16**.

Урок 5

Pairs of Vowels: Ы - И

Ы   ⟶   И

мы́ло

Ми́ла

Упражнение 21

17

Listen to the audio and repeat syllables with hard and soft vowels after the native speaker.

мы – ми;   зы – зи;   ты – ти;   вы – ви;   сы – си;   ры – ри.

Упражнение 22

18

Listen to the words with hard and soft vowels and repeat after the native speaker.

1. мы́ло – Ми́ла;   2. ты – тигр;   3. Зи́на – му́зыка;   4. ры́ба – риск;

5. вы – Ви́ктор;   6. сыр;   7. цветы́;   8. кондиционе́р;   9. ли́лия;   10. кио́ск.

Какая мышь большая?

Это мышь, и это то́же мышь.

Это бе́лая мышь, а это се́рая мышь.

Кака́я мышь больша́я: белая или серая?

Белая мышь большая, а серая – маленькая.

 Упражнение 23

Create three sentences to each set of words, as in the example.

1. лимо́н (жёлтый, зелёный)   **Это лимон, и это тоже лимон.   Это жёлтый**

   лимон, а это зелёный лимон. Жёлтый лимон большой, а зелёный –

   маленький. _____

2. я́блоко (кра́сный, жёлтый) _____

   _____

   _____

3. кни́га (си́ний, бе́лый) _____

   _____

   _____

4. шокола́д (бе́лый, чёрный) _____

_____

_____

5. ры́ба (си́ний, ро́зовый) _____

_____

_____

6. такси́ (жёлтый, се́рый) _____

_____

_____

7. лилия (белый, жёлтый) _____

_____

_____

8. стул (зелёный, чёрный) _____

_____

_____

And now please work with audio **Track 19**.

Цвет

Color the cells of the table accordingly.

голубой цвет	оранжевый цвет	коричневый цвет	фиолетовый цвет

Вот здесь – вон там

- Где чай?

- Он вон там.

- Там какой чай?

- Там чёрный чай.

- А где ваза: там или здесь?

- Она вот здесь, справа.

- Где телефон?

- Телефон вот здесь, слева.

- А где книга?

- Книга тоже вот здесь, слева.

And now please work with audio **Tracks 20 - 21**.

Упражнение 24

Look at the picture on the next page and answer questions about the near and distant objects, following the example.

Образец: 1. **Нет он не вот здесь слева. Он вон там слева.**

1. Мобильный телефон вот здесь слева 2. Ручка вон там справа? 3. Сыр вот здесь слева? 4. Зелёный чай вот здесь, слева? 5. Русская книга вот здесь слева? 6. Цветы вон там, справа? 7. Рыба вот здесь слева? 8. Белая лилия вот здесь слева? 9. Мандарин вон там слева? 10. Борщ вот здесь справа? 11. Яблоко вон там справа? 12. Хлеб вон там справа? 13. Стул вот здесь слева? 14. Ёлка вот здесь справа? 15. Клубника вон там слева? 16. Пицца вон там справа?

вон там

слева

справа

вот здесь

Урок 6

Unstressed O

O - A

Это авока́до.

Это оте́ц и сын.

 Упражнение 25

 `22`

Read the following words, then listen to the audio and repeat after the native speaker. Consult the dictionary if you need help with translation. Write the words down with the stress mark.

1. домино __домино́_____

2. администратор _____

3. профессия _____

4. очки _____

5. большой _____

6. доктор _____

7. один _____

8. команда _____

9. собака _____

10. отец _____

11. зовут _____

12. полиция _____

13. Россия _____

14. робот _____

Семья

Знако́мьтесь,

это Оля Па́влова.

Она шко́льница.

Это папа.

Его зовут Никола́й Иванович Па́влов.

Он инжене́р.

Это мама,

Её зовут Ири́на Алекса́ндровна Па́влова.

Ирина Александровна тоже инженер?

Нет, она не инженер.

А кто она?

Она учи́тельница.

Это ста́рший брат, Ди́ма Па́влов.

Дима шко́льник?

Нет, он не школьник. Он студе́нт.

And now please work with audio **Tracks 23 - 24**.

Упражнение 26

Write down the last name of each man's wife. Practice reading Russian names. Pay attention to the stress mark.

1. Андре́й Гра́дов (Ни́на) **Жена – Нина Градова**

2. Ива́н Петро́в (Татья́на) _____

3. Влади́мир Му́хин (Людми́ла) _____

4. Серге́й Медве́дев (Светла́на) _____

5. Бори́с Си́доров (Ни́на) _____

6. Фёдор Достое́вский (А́нна) _____

7. Лев Толсто́й (Со́фья) _____

8. Васи́лий Чайко́вский (Алекса́ндра) _____

ФИО

фамилия, имя, отчество		
отец	сын	дочь
Пётр Степанович Иванов	Дмитрий **Петрович** Иванов	Маргарита **Петровна** Иванов**а**
Василий Михайлович Курников	Сергей **Васильевич** Курников	Юлия **Васильевна** Курников**а**
Андрей Алексеевич Зайцев	Борис **Андреевич** Зайцев	Мария **Андреевна** Зайцев**а**
Семён Степанович Белый	Максим **Семёнович** Белый	Галина **Семёновна** Бела**я**

Упражнение 27

Write down the names of each man's children, as in the example.

1. Оте́ц – Пётр Андре́евич Гра́дов (Влади́мир, Ни́на) __**Сын – Владимир Петрович Градов. Дочь – Нина Петровна Градова.**__

2. Отец – Серге́й Васи́льевич Ко́нев (Андре́й, Ю́лия) _____

    _____

    _____

3. Отец – Пётр Серге́евич Горбачёв (Ива́н, Ири́на) _____

    _____

    _____

4. Отец – Алексе́й Макси́мович Иванов (Максим, Анна) _____

    _____

    _____

5. Отец – Иван Васильевич Чонкин (Глеб, Татья́на) _____

    _____

    _____

6. Отец – Никола́й Ива́нович Па́влов (Дми́трий, О́льга) _____

    _____

    _____

7. Отец – Алекса́ндр Серге́евич Пу́шкин (Алекса́ндр, Ната́лья) _____

    _____

    _____

8. Отец – Семён Васи́льевич Горбунко́в (Семён, Мария) _____

    _____

_____

9. Отец – Андре́й Никола́евич Круто́й (Серге́й, Еле́на) _____

_____

_____

10. Отец – Виктор Альбертович Михайлов (Виталий, Анна) _____

_____

And now please work with audio **Track 25**.

Упражнение 28

Please calculate and write down answers, following the example.

1) 11 + 2 = _____**Одиннадцать плюс два будет тринадцать.**_____

2) 17 − 1 = _____

3) 20 − 6 = _____

4) 10 + 9 = _____

5) 18 − 17 = _____

6) 16 − 4 = _____

7) 14 + 4 = _____

8) 8 + 8 = _____

9) 19 - 19 = _____

And now please work with audio **Track 26**.

Grammar and Translation

Lesson 1

Vowels

There are ten vowels in the Russian alphabet that can be divided into five pairs which make similar sounds.

Hard Vowels		Soft Vowels
А	⟶	Я [йа]
Э	⟶	Е [йе]
О	⟶	Ё [йо]
У	⟶	Ю [йю]
Ы	⟶	И

The first four pairs of vowels make really similar sounds: one is harder, the other is softer. The soft vowel in each pair is made up of two sounds heard together: й + hard vowel. Listen to the audio and hear the difference between the hard and the soft vowels.

Soft Vowels

Usually students don't have any problems with hard vowels. They are easy to understand.

But! with the soft vowels you have to memorize a couple of rules.

Rule № 1 A soft vowel sounds exactly like it does in the alphabet when it is preceded by another vowel or is at the beginning of a word (two sounds).

> **Юлия** [йулийа] - all of the vowels in this word are pronounced as in the alphabet. The letter **Ю** is at the beginning of the word. The letter **я** is preceded by another vowel (**и**).

Rule № 2 When a soft vowel is preceded by a consonant, it makes the preceding consonant soft, and it makes only one sound instead of two.

> Ляля [ляля] — each letter **я** in this word makes only one soft sound.

In this lesson we will practice the first pair of vowels: **а — я**.

Formal and Informal Names

English speaking people use short forms of names to address people: Debby or Deb for Deborah, Joe for Joseph, Bob for Robert, etc. Russians widely use informal names in families and with friends. These informal names are sometimes longer than the corresponding formal names.

Here are some examples of Russian informal names.

Formal and Informal Names

Formal Name	Informal Name
Татья́на	Та́ня, Та́нечка, Таню́ша
О́льга	О́ля, О́лечка
Ната́лья	Ната́ша, Ната́шенька
Мари́я	Ма́ша, Ма́шенька, Мару́ся
Алекса́ндр, Александра	Са́ша, Са́шенька, Шу́ра
Ива́н	Ва́ня, Ва́нечка, Ваню́ша
Влади́мир	Воло́дя, Во́ва, Во́вка
Дми́трий	Ди́ма, Димо́н, Ди́мочка

Be Polite

As mentioned earlier, there are two forms of addressing people: informal **ты** and polite **вы** in Russian. With **ты** we address children. People of the same age can address each other with **ты** too, if they agreed on that earlier[1]. The same rule applies when it comes to greetings.

Здравствуйте! = *Hello!* - polite

Здравствуй! = *Hello!* - informal

Привет! = *Hi!* - informal

---

[1] Usually adults of the same age address each other with **вы** when they meet for the first time. Then they can agree to switch to the informal **ты**.

We say **здравствуйте** to adults or to a group of people (more than one person).

We say **здравствуй** to children or people of the same age if agreed upon earlier.

We also use informal forms of greetings and addressing with our close relatives: mother, father, grandmother, grandfather. We can also use this forms with other relatives: uncle, aunts, etc., depending on the closeness of your relationship with them.

Remember: you never say **Здравствуй!** or **Привет!** to your teacher – it's impolite.

You should say **Здравствуйте!**

What is Your Name?/Translation

Здравствуйте, я Иван. = *Hello, I am Ivan.*

Меня зовут Иван. = *My name is Ivan.*

Ты Оля. = *You are Olya.*

Тебя зовут Оля. = *Your name is Olya.*

Вы Светлана. = *You are Svetlana.*

Вас зовут Светлана. = *Your name is Svetlana.*

Мы Антон и Нина. = *We are Anton and Nina.*

Нас зовут Антон и Нина. = *Our names are Anton and Nina.*

Lesson 2

Masculine and Feminine Adjectives

A noun is a word that names a thing: a person, a place, an idea, etc.:

кот = *a cat*   человек = *a person*   море = *sea*

An adjective is a word that describes a noun (color, size, quality):

большой = *big*   красный = *red*   хороший = *good*

As you already know, every Russian noun has a gender. There are three genders in Russian: masculine, feminine, and neuter.

The Russian adjective agrees with the noun that it describes. It has a different ending depending on the gender of the noun. In this lesson we will learn the adjective endings for masculine and feminine nouns.

Masculine and Feminine Adjectives

он	она
как**ой**?	как**ая**?
бе́л**ый**	бе́л**ая**
си́н**ий**	си́н**яя**
больш**о́й**	больш**а́я**

Какой?

The word **какой** is a very useful word.

We use it when we want to ask about the size, quality, color, brand, etc. As you see from the table, the question word also agrees with the noun it describes.

Translation of the New Vocabulary

Кто это? = *Who is this?*

Это девочка. = *This is a girl.*

Какая это девочка? = *What can you say about this girl? = What kind of a girl is she?*

Это умная девочка. = *This is a smart girl.*

Какой это телефон? = *What kind of a phone is this?*

Это хороший телефон. = *This is a good phone.*

Какая это снежинка? = *What can you say about this snowflake?*

Это холодная снежинка. = *This is a cold snowflake.*

большой мяч = *a big ball*   маленькая ручка = *a small pen*

весёлый мальчик = *a joyful boy*   добрая бабушка = *a kind grandma*

красивый цветок = *a beautiful flower*

Lesson 3

Neuter Adjectives

In the previous lesson we learned the adjective endings for masculine and feminine objects. Let's learn adjective's endings for neuter objects.

Яблоко красное. = *The apple is red.*

Море синее. = *The sea is blue.*

Masculine, Feminine, and Neuter Adjectives

он	она	оно
как**ой**?	как**ая**?	как**ое**?
бе́л**ый**	бе́л**ая**	бел**ое**
си́н**ий**	си́н**яя**	син**ее**
больш**о́й**	больш**а́я**	больш**ое**

Translation of the New Vocabulary

Что это? = *What is this?*

Это клубника. = *This is a strawberry.*

Какого она цвета? = *What color is it?*

Она красная. = *It is red.*

Что это такое? = *What is this?*

Это огурец. = *This is a cucumber.*

Какого цвета огурец? = *What color is the cucumber?*

Огурец зелёный. = *The cucumber is green.*

Lesson 4

Over Here/Right/Left

Just as in English, there are different ways to talk about near objects in Russian.

здесь = *here*   справа = *on the right*

вот = *here* (when pointing)   слева = *on the left*

вот здесь = *over here*

More Personal Pronouns

In lesson 1 we learned the introduction dialogue with four personal pronouns: **меня, тебя, нас, вас**.

Let's learn the rest of them:

я	ты	мы	вы	он	она	они
зовут							
меня	тебя	нас	вас	его	её	их

Он Дмитрий. Его зовут Дмитрий. = *He is Dmitry. His name is Dmitry.*

Она Рита. Её зовут Рита. = *She is Rita. Her name is Rita.*

Они Саша и Паша. Их зовут Саша и Паша. = *They are Sasha and Pasha. Their names are Sasha and Pasha.*

Translation of the New Vocabulary

Где петух? = *Where is the rooster?*

Он вот здесь слева. = *It's over here on the left.*

А где змея? = *And where is the snake?*

Она вот здесь справа. = *It is over here on the right.*

Какого цвета слон? = *What color is the elephant?*

Он серый. = *It is gray.*

Кто ещё серый? = *What else is gray?*

Ёж. Ёж тоже серый. = *The hedgehog. The hedgehog is also gray.*

Сколько будет…? = *What is…?*

Один плюс три будет четыре. = *One plus three equals four. (Literally: One plus three will be four.)*

Семь минус пять будет два. = *Seven minus five equals two.*

Lesson 5

Which Mouse Is Big? / Translation

Это мышь, и это тоже мышь. = *This is a mouse, and this is also a mouse.*

Это белая мышь, а это серая мышь. = *This is a white mouse, and this is a gray mouse.*

Какая мышь большая: белая или серая? = *Which mouse is big: the white one or the gray one?*

Белая мышь большая, а серая мышь маленькая. = *The white mouse is big, and the gray one is small.*

Over Here/Over There

There are different ways to talk about distant objects in Russian.

здесь = *here*	там = *there*
вот = *here* (when pointing)	вон = *there* (when pointing)
вот здесь = *over here*	вон там = *over there*

Where Is the Object? / Translation

Где чай? = *Where is the tea?*

Он вон там. = *It's over there.*

Там какой чай? = *What kind of tea is there?* (Literally: There what tea?)

Там чёрный чай. = *That's black tea there.*

А где ваза: там или здесь? = *And where is the vase: there or here?*

Она вот здесь, справа. = *It's over here on the right.*

Где телефон? = *Where is the phone?*

Телефон вот здесь, слева. = *The phone is right here on the left.*

А где книга? = *And where is the book?*

Книга тоже вот здесь, слева. = *The book is also over here on the left.*

Usually the word order does not matter in Russian.

Чёрный чай там. = Там чёрный чай.

Lesson 6

Unstressed O

In the Workbook 1 you already learned that unstressed **O** is pronounced as **A** in all Russian words.

авока́до = [авакада]

In the word **авокадо** the stress falls on the letter **A**, therefore all letters **O** are pronounced as **A**.

Family / Translation

There are two different words to describe students in school and in college. Therefore, we will use *schoolboy* and a *schoolgirl to indicate school students (K – 12) and the word student for the college or university students.*

Знакомьтесь. Это Оля Павлова = *Let me introduce Olya Pavlova.*

Она школьница = *She is a schoolgirl.*

Это папа, Николай Павлов = *This is her dad, Nikolay Pavlov.*
Он инженер. = *He is an engineer.*

Это мама, Ирина Павлова =*This is her mom, Irina Pavlova.*
Она учительница. = *She is a teacher.*

Это старший брат, Дима Павлов. = *This is her older brother, Dima Pavlov.*
Дима школьник? = *Is Dima a schoolboy?*
Нет, он не школьник. Он студент. = *No, he is not a schoolboy. He is a student.*

Кто это? = *Who is this?*

Last Name

The last name's ending changes according to the gender of the person.

The male's last name ends in a consonant and a female's last name ends in **a**. Usually the wife takes her husband's last name.

First and Last Names

он	она
Михайл Ивано́в	О́льга Ивано́в**а**
Пётр Цветко́в	Ирина Цветко́в**а**
Андре́й Фоми́н	Мари́я Фомина́
И́горь Круто́й	Мари́на Крут**а́я**

If a male's last name is an adjective, the corresponding female's name follows the rule of adjectives (See Adjectives).

Крут**ой** is an adjective. It means steep. So, for a female it changes to Крут**ая**.

Very often a last name derives from the first name (as in English).

Jack ⟶ Jackson   John ⟶ Johnson

In this case a male name has the **-ов/ев** ending.

For example:

Иван ⟶ Иван**о́в**   Алексей ⟶ Алексе́**ев**

Patronymic

The patronymic name is based on one's father's first name. If the father's name has the **-ь** or **-й** at the end, the patronymic has the **-евич** ending for a male and **-евна** for a female. In the rest of the cases, most of the time the patronymic has the **-ович** ending for male and **-овна** for female.

Patronymic

Father's Name	Son's Patronymic	Daughter's Patronymic
Ива́н	Ива́**нович**	Ива́**новна**
Андре́**й**	Андре́**евич**	Андре́**евна**
Влади́мир	Влади́мир**ович**	Влади́мир**овна**

The patronymic is always used together with the formal first name (never with the informal one).

Ольга Ивановна   Ирина Александровна

Which Name to Use and When

First + patronymic is used:

1) with a teacher

2) in a business settings

The **first** name is used to address children and in many other cases that are not listed above. To be on the safe side, you should use the name with which the person first was introduced to you.

Usually, children are addressed by their informal names.

Answer Key

Ответы

Упражнение 3

Boys: Степан – Стёпа, Иван – Ваня, Пётр – Петя, Виктор –Витя, Борис – Боря, Александр – Саша, Михаил – Миша, Николай – Коля, Антон – Антоша, Алексей – Лёша;

Girls: Дарья – Даша, Мария – Маша, Марина – Мариша, Александра – Саша, Лариса – Лара, Нина – Ниночка, Наталья – Наташа, Ольга – Оля, Светлана – Света, Маргарита – Рита.

Упражнение 4

2. Здравствуйте, Мария.   3. Здравствуйте, Виктор.   4. Здравствуй, Иван. 5. Здравствуйте, доктор. 6. Здравствуй, бабушка. (If this is your grandma) Здравствуйте, бабушка. (If it is not your grandma)

Упражнение 5

2. Как вас зовут? Вас зовут Ирина. 3. Как меня зовут? Меня зовут Антон. 4. Как нас зовут? Нас зовут Нина и Зина. 5. Как меня зовут? Меня зовут Маргарита. 6. Как вас зовут? Вас зовут Линда. 7. Как тебя зовут? Тебя зовут Том. 8 Как тебя зовут? Тебя зовут Моника. 9. Как нас зовут? Нас зовут Маша и Даша. 10. Как тебя зовут? Тебя зовут Аня.

Упражнение 8

2. Какой это ресторан? Это хороший ресторан. 3. Какая это книга? Это хорошая книга. 4. Какая это галерея? Это хорошая галерея. 5. Какой это парк? Это хороший парк. 6. Какая это балерина? Это хорошая балерина. 7. Какой это шоколад? Это хороший шоколад. 8. Какой это мяч? Это хороший мяч. 9. Какая это спортсменка?

Это хорошая спортсменка.   10. Какой это мальчик? Это хороший мальчик.
11. Какая это ёлка? Это хорошая ёлка.

Упражнение 9

2. Это Анна. Она красивая.   3. Это президент. Он умный.   4. Это ресторан. Он хороший. 5. Это бабушка. Она добрая. 6. Это стол. Он большой. 7. Это каска. Она маленькая. 8. Это собака. Она умная. 9. Это журнал. Он интересный.

Упражнение 13

2. Нет, море не красное. Море синее. 3. Нет, лампа не чёрная. Лампа белая. 4. Нет, авокадо не белое. Авокадо зелёное. 5. Нет, ручка не зелёная. Ручка чёрная. 6. Нет, бумага не красная. Бумага синяя. 7. Нет, крокодил не белый. Крокодил зелёный.

Упражнение 14

2. Какого цвета компьютер? Он чёрный.   3. Какого цвета такси? Оно синее.
4. Какого цвета меню? Оно белое. 5. Какого цвета огурец? Он зелёный. 6. Какого цвета роза? Она красная.   7. Какого цвета лилия? Она синяя.   8. Какого цвета молоко? Оно белое. 9. Какого цвета борщ? Он красный. 10. Какого цвета ёлка? Она зелёная. 11. Какого цвета свитер? Он синий. 12. Какого цвета лимон? Он жёлтый.

Упражнение 15

12 –двенадцать;   13 – тринадцать;   14 – четырнадцать;   15 – пятнадцать;   16 – шестнадцать;   17 – семнадцать;   18 – восемнадцать;   19 – девятнадцать;   20 – двадцать.

Упражнение 18

2. Он вот здесь справа. 3. Он вот здесь слева. 4. Он вот здесь справа. 5. Он вот здесь справа. 6. Он вот здесь справа. 7. Он вот здесь слева. 8. Она вот здесь слева. 9. Он вот здесь слева. 10. Она вот здесь слева. 11. Она вот здесь слева. 12. Он вот здесь слева. 13. Она вот здесь справа.

Упражнение 19

2. Как её зовут? Её зовут Марина. 3. Как меня зовут? Меня зовут Маргарита. 4. Как их зовут? Их зовут Зоя и Ира. 5. Как нас зовут? Нас зовут Ольга и Дмитрий. 6. Как вас зовут? Вас зовут Наташа. 7. Как тебя зовут? Тебя зовут Джон. 8. Как его зовут? Его зовут Джеймс. 9. Как её зовут? Её зовут Настя. 10. Как его зовут? Его зовут Степан. 11. Как её зовут? Её зовут Тамара. 12. Как их зовут? Их зовут Николай и Виктор.

Упражнение 20

2. Семь минус один будет шесть. 3. Десять минус пять будет пять. 4. Девять плюс девять будет восемнадцать. 5. Шестнадцать минус два будет четырнадцать. 6. Семнадцать минус один будет шестнадцать. 7. Двадцать минус пять будет пятнадцать. 8. Восемь плюс один будет девять. 9. Девятнадцать минус один будет восемнадцать.

Упражнение 23

2. Это яблоко, и это тоже яблоко. Это красное яблоко, а это жёлтое яблоко. Красное яблоко большое, а жёлтое – маленькое. 3. Это книга, и это тоже книга. Это синяя книга, а это белая книга. Синяя книга большая, а белая – маленькая. 4. Это шоколад, и это тоже шоколад. Это белый шоколад, а это чёрный шоколад. Белый шоколад большой, а чёрный – маленький. 5. Это рыба, и это тоже рыба. Это синяя рыба, а это розовая рыба. Синяя рыба большая, а розовая – маленькая. 6. Это такси, и это тоже такси. Это жёлтое такси, а это серое такси. Жёлтое такси большое, а серое – маленькое. 7. Это лилия, и это тоже лилия. Это белая лилия, а это жёлтая лилия. Белая лилия большая, а жёлтая – маленькая. 8. Это стул, и это тоже стул. Это зелёный стул, а это чёрный стул. Зелёный стул большой, а чёрный – маленький.

Упражнение 24

2. Нет, она не вон там справа. Она вот здесь справа. 3. Нет, он не вот здесь слева. Он вон там слева. 4. Нет, он не вот здесь слева. Она вон там справа. 5. Нет, она не вот здесь слева. Она вот здесь справа. 6. Нет, они не вон там справа. Они вот здесь справа. 7. Да, она вот здесь слева. 8. Нет, она не вот здесь слева. Она вон там

справа. 9. Да, он вон там слева. 10. Нет, он не вот здесь справа. Он вон там слева. 11. Нет, оно не вон там справа. Оно вот здесь слева. 12. Нет, он не вон там справа. Он вот здесь справа. 13. Да, он вот здесь слева. 14. Нет, она не вот здесь справа. Она вот здесь слева. 15. Нет, она не вон там слева. Она вон там справа. 16. Да, она вон там справа.

Упражнение 25

2. администра́тор; 3. профе́ссия; 4. очки́; 5. большо́й; 6. до́ктор; 7. оди́н; 8. кома́нда; 9. соба́ка; 10. оте́ц; 11. зову́т; 12. поли́ция; 13. Росси́я; 14. ро́бот.

Упражнение 26

2. Жена – Татьяна Петрова. 3. Жена – Людмила Мухина. 4. Жена – Светлана Медведева. 5. Жена – Нина Сидорова. 6. Жена – Анна Достоевская. 7. Жена – Софья Толстая. 8. Жена – Александра Чайковская.

Упражнение 27

2. Сын - Андрей Сергеевич Конев. Дочь - Юлия Сергеевна Конева. 3. Сын - Иван Петрович Горбачёв. Дочь - Ирина Петровна Горбачёва. 4. Сын - Максим Алексеевич Иванов. Дочь - Анна Алексеевна Иванова. 5. Сын - Глеб Иванович Чонкин. Дочь - Татьяна Ивановна Чонкина. 6. Дмитрий Николаевич Павлов. Дочь - Ольга Николаевна Павлова. 7. Сын - Александр Александрович Пушкин. Дочь - Наталья Александровна Пушкина. 8. Сын - Семён Семёнович Горбунков. Дочь - Мария Семёновна Горбункова. 9. Сын - Сергей Андреевич Крутой. Дочь - Елена Андреевна Крутая. 10. Сын - Виталий Викторович Михайлов. Дочь - Анна Викторовна Михайлова.

Упражнение 28

2. Семнадцать минус один будет шестнадцать. 3. Двадцать минус шесть будет четырнадцать. 4. Десять плюс девять будет девятнадцать. 5. Восемнадцать минус семнадцать будет один. 6. Шестнадцать минус четыре будет двенадцать. 7. Четырнадцать плюс четыре будет восемнадцать. 8. Восемь плюс восемь будет шестнадцать. 9. Девятнадцать минус девятнадцать будет ноль.

Audio Script

Урок 1

1 Урок номер один. Упражнение один. Слушайте и повторяйте!

ба – бя;   ла – ля;   да – дя;   на – ня;   са – ся;   ра – ря;

2 Упражнение два. Слушайте и повторяйте!

Банк – бяка;   Лариса – Ляля;   брат – ряд;   Саша – Вася;   Нина – няня;

матч – мяч; дама – дядя; такси - тётя; опера – наряд;   Шура – Боря.

3 Упражнение 5. Слушайте и отвечайте!

Ты Саша. Как тебя зовут? Тебя зовут Саша.

Вы Ирина. Как вас зовут? Вас зовут Ирина.

Я Антон. Как меня зовут? Меня зовут Антон.

Мы Нина и Зина. Как нас зовут? Нас зовут Нина и Зина.

Я Маргарита. Как меня зовут? Меня зовут Маргарита.

Вы Линда. Как вас зовут? Вас зовут Линда.

Ты Том. Как тебя зовут? Тебя зовут Том.

Ты Моника. Как тебя зовут? Тебя зовут Моника.

Мы Маша и Даша. Как нас зовут? Нас зовут Маша и Даша.

Ты Аня. Как тебя зовут? Тебя зовут Аня.

Хорошо!

Урок 2

4

Урок номер два. Упражнение шесть. Слушайте и повторяйте!

мэ – ме;   лэ – ле;   тэ – те;   нэ – не;   сэ – се;   рэ – ре;

Хорошо!

5

Упражнение семь. Слушайте и повторяйте!

Меня;   тебя;   Мэри;   телефон;   проблема;   Дэвид;   галерея;   интернет; инженер;   балерина;   каратэ;   момент.

Хорошо!

6

Упражнение восемь. Слушайте и отвечайте!

Это лампа. Какая это лампа? Это хорошая лампа.

Это ресторан. Какой это ресторан? Это хороший ресторан.

Это книга. Какая это книга? Это хорошая книга.

Это галерея. Какая это галерея? Это хорошая галерея.

Это парк. Какой это парк? Это хороший парк.

Это балерина. Какая это балерина? Это хорошая балерина.

Это шоколад. Какой это шоколад? Это хороший шоколад.

Это мяч. Какой это мяч? Это хороший мяч.

Это спортсменка. Какая это спортсменка? Это хорошая спортсменка.

Это мальчик. Какой это мальчик? Это хороший мальчик.

Это ёлка. Какая это ёлка? Это хорошая ёлка.

Очень хорошо!

7

Упражнение девять. Поговорим!

сок/холодный: Это сок. Он холодный.

Анна/красивый: Это Анна. Она красивая.

президент/умный: Это президент. Он умный.

ресторан/хороший: Это ресторан. Он хороший.

бабушка/добрый: Это бабушка. Она добрая.

стол/большой: Это стол. Он большой.

каска/маленький: Это каска. Она маленькая.

журнал/интересный: Это журнал. Он интересный.

Хорошо!

8 Посчитаем! Слушайте и повторяйте!

одиннадцать; двенадцать; тринадцать; четырнадцать; пятнадцать; шестнадцать; семнадцать; восемнадцать; девятнадцать; двадцать.

Отлично!

Урок 3

9 Урок номер три

Упражнение одиннадцать. Слушайте и повторяйте!

во – вё; мо – мё; ло – лё; то – тё; но – нё; со – сё; ро – рё.

Очень хорошо!

10

Упражнение двенадцать. Слушайте и повторяйте!

Антон – Стёпа;   Лора – Лёша;   Том – тётя;   сок – весёлый;   Боря – ребёнок;   Зоя – козёл;   мост – мёд;   нос;   самолёт;   актёр.

Хорошо!

11

Слушайте и повторяйте!

Цвет: белый цвет, чёрный цвет, красный цвет, жёлтый цвет, зелёный цвет, синий цвет.

Хорошо!

12

Слушайте и отвечайте!

Банан синий или жёлтый? Банан жёлтый.

Море синее или красное? Море синее.

Авокадо белое или зелёное? Авокадо зелёное.

Крокодил белый или зелёный? Крокодил зелёный.

Яблоко красное или чёрное? Яблоко красное.

Пингвин жёлтый или чёрный? Пингвин чёрный.

Очень хорошо!

13

Слушайте и отвечайте!

Солнце синее? Нет, оно не синее. Какого оно цвета? Солнце жёлтое.

Ёлка белая? Нет, она не белая. Какого она цвета? Ёлка зелёная.

Огурец красный? Нет, он не красный. Какого он цвета? Огурец зелёный.

Море жёлтое? Нет, оно не жёлтое. Какого оно цвета? Море синее.

Лимон белый? Нет, он не белый. Какого он цвета? Лимон жёлтый.

Молоко чёрное? Нет, оно не чёрное. Какого оно цвета? Молоко белое.

Отлично!

Урок 4

14 Урок номер четыре. Упражнение шестнадцать. Слушайте и повторяйте!

му – мю;   лу – лю;   ту – тю;   ну – ню;   су – сю;   ру – рю.

Хорошо!

15 Упражнение семнадцать. Слушайте и повторяйте!

музыка – мюсли;   спутник – пюре;   лук – люк;   турист – костюм;   ручка – брюки;   Людмила;   студент;   Тимур.

Хорошо!

16 Слушайте и отвечайте!

Сколько будет один плюс три? Один плюс три будет четыре.

Сколько будет семь минус пять? Семь минус пять будет два.

Сколько будет два плюс шесть? Два плюс шесть будет восемь.

Сколько будет десять минус один? Десять минус один будет девять.

Сколько будет семь минус семь? Семь минус семь будет ноль.

Сколько будет десять плюс десять? Десять плюс десять будет двадцать.

Сколько будет девять минус пять? Девять минус пять будет четыре.

Отлично!

Урок 5

17

Урок номер пять. Упражнение двадцать один. Слушайте и повторяйте!

мы – ми; зы – зи; ты – ти; вы – ви; сы – си; ры – ри.

Хорошо!

18

Упражнение двадцать два. Слушайте и повторяйте!

мы – Мила; ты – тигр; Зина – музыка; рыба – риск; вы – Виктор; сыр;

цветы; кондиционер; лилия; киоск.

Хорошо!

19

Слушайте и отвечайте!

слон/ёж: Кто большой, а кто маленький? Слон большой, а ёж маленький.

солнце/море: Что жёлтое, а что синее? Солнце жёлтое, а море синее.

яблоко/шоколад: Что красное, а что чёрное? Яблоко красное, а шоколад чёрный.

авокадо/лимон: Что зелёное, а что жёлтое? Авокадо зелёное, а лимон жёлтый.

пантера/крокодил: Кто чёрный, а кто зелёный? Пантера чёрная, а крокодил зелёный.

Отлично!

20

Слушайте!

- Где чай?

- Он вон там.

- Там какой чай?

-Там чёрный чай.

-А где ваза: там или здесь?

- Она вот здесь справа.

- Где телефон?

- Телефон вот здесь, слева.

- А где книга?

- Книга тоже вот здесь, слева.

21 А теперь слушайте и повторяйте!

- Где чай?

- Он вон там.

- Там какой чай?

-Там чёрный чай.

-А где ваза: там или здесь?

- Она вот здесь справа.

- Где телефон?

- Телефон вот здесь, слева.

- А где книга?

- Книга тоже вот здесь, слева.

Очень хорошо!

Урок 6

22 Урок номер шесть. Упражнение двадцать пять. Слушайте и повторяйте!

Домино, администратор, профессия, очки, большой, доктор, один, команда, собака, отец, зовут, полиция, Россия, робот.

Хорошо!

23 Слушайте!

Семья. Знакомьтесь, это Оля Павлова. Она школьница. Это папа, Николай Иванович Павлов. Он инженер. Это мама, Ирина Александровна Павлова. Она учительница. Это старший брат, Дима Павлов. Дима школьник? Нет, он не школьник. Он студент.

24 А теперь слушайте и отвечайте!

Ирина Александровна дизайнер? Нет, она не дизайнер.

А кто она? Она учительница.

Николай Иванович инженер? Да, он инженер.

Дима Павлов школьник? Нет, он не школьник.

А кто он? Он студент.

Очень хорошо!

25 Поговорим!

Здравствуйте, я Юля. Мой отец Сергей Васильевич Конев. Меня зовут … Меня зовут Юлия Сергеевна Конева.

Здравствуйте, я Иван. Мой отец Пётр Сергеевич Горбачёв. Меня зовут … Меня зовут Иван Петрович Горбачёв.

Здравствуйте, я Наташа. Мой отец Николай Иванович Лобов. Меня зовут … Меня зовут Наталья Николаевна Лобова.

Здравствуйте, я Дима Павлов. Мой отец Николай Иванович Павлов. Меня зовут … Меня зовут Дмитрий Николаевич Павлов.

Здравствуйте, я Ирина. Мой отец Игорь Борисович Крутой. Меня зовут … Меня зовут Ирина Игоревна Крутая.

Здравствуйте, я Сергей. Мой отец Александр Сергеевич Петров. Меня зовут. … Меня зовут Сергей Александрович Петров.

Хорошо!

26 Упражнение двадцать восемь. Посчитаем!

Сколько будет одиннадцать плюс два? Одиннадцать плюс два будет тринадцать.

Сколько будет семнадцать минус один? Семнадцать минус один будет шестнадцать.

Сколько будет двадцать минус шесть? Двадцать минус шесть будет четырнадцать.

Сколько будет десять плюс девять? Десять плюс девять будет девятнадцать.

Сколько будет восемнадцать минус семнадцать? Восемнадцать минус семнадцать будет один.

Сколько будет шестнадцать минус четыре? Шестнадцать минус четыре будет двенадцать.

Сколько будет четырнадцать плюс четыре? Четырнадцать плюс четыре будет восемнадцать.

Сколько будет восемь плюс восемь? Восемь плюс восемь будет шестнадцать.

Сколько будет девятнадцать минус девятнадцать? Девятнадцать минус девятнадцать будет ноль.

Отлично!

Grammar Tables

Personal Pronouns

Кто?						
я	ты	вы	мы	он	она	они
зовут						
меня	тебя	вас	нас	его	её	их

Numbers

0	1	2	3	4
ноль	один	два	три	четыре
5	6	7	8	9
пять	шесть	семь	восемь	девять
10	11	12	13	14
десять	одиннадцать	двенадцать	тринадцать	четырнадцать
15	16	17	18	19
пятнадцать	шестнадцать	семнадцать	восемнадцать	девятнадцать
20				
двадцать				

Adjective Declensions

он	она	оно
-ой -ый -ий	**-ая -яя**	**-ое -ее**
больш**ой**	больш**ая**	больш**ое**
маленьк**ий**	маленьк**ая**	маленьк**ое**
бел**ый**	бел**ая**	бел**ое**
син**ий**	син**яя**	син**ее**

Dictionaries

Russian - English Dictionary

Every time a noun ends in a soft sign or has an irregular ending for the certain gender it is indicated by:

m - masculine   *f* – feminine   *n* - neuter

А

а   and, but, oh, so
абрико́с   apricot
авока́до   avocado
авто́бус   bus
администра́ция   administration
а́дрес   address
аква́риум   aquarium
актёр   actor
актри́са   actress
алфави́т   alphabet
Аме́рика   America
А́нглия   England
анекдо́т   anecdote, funny story
апельси́н   *n*   orange
А́фрика   Africa
аэропо́рт   airport

Б

ба́бушка   grandmother
бага́ж   baggage
бадминто́н   badminton
бале́т   ballet
балери́на   ballerina
балко́н   balcony
бана́н   banana
банк   bank
бар   bar
баскетбо́л   basketball

бе́лый   white
библиоте́ка   library
бизнесме́н   businessman
бокс   boxing
большо́й   big
борщ   beet (beetroot) soup
босс   boss
бота́ника   botany
брасле́т   bracelet
брат   brother
брю́ки   pants
буке́т   bouquet
бума́га   paper

В

ва́за   vase
ве́щь   belonging, stuff, thing
вода́   water
вон   there
   вон там   over there
вопро́с   question, problem, issue
восемна́дцать   eighteen
во́семь   eight
вот   here
   вот здесь   over here
врач   doctor
въезд   entrance (for vehicles)
вы   you (polite *sing/pl*)

Г

галере́я gallery
гара́ж garage
где where
геогра́фия geography
гео́лог geologist
Герма́ния Germany
геро́й hero
гимна́стика gymnastics
голубо́й sky blue
гость *m* guest
гото́в *sfa* is ready
грамм gram
гру́ппа group

Д

да yes
два́дцать twenty
двена́дцать twelve
дверь *f* door
де́вочка little girl
девятна́дцать nineteen
де́вять nine
де́душка grandfather
де́ло business
день *m* day
де́рево tree
десе́рт dessert
де́сять ten
джéмпер pullover
джи́нсы jeans
диало́г dialogue
дипло́м diploma
дире́ктор director
диск disk
до́брый kind
дождь *m* rain
до́ктор doctor
докуме́нт document
до́ллар dollar
дом house, building

дочь daughter
друг friend
дя́дя uncle

Е

ещё still, yet, more
её her
его́ him

Ё

ёж hedgehog
ёлка fir tree

Ж

жена́ wife
жёлтый yellow
жира́ф giraffe
жук beetle
журна́л *n* magazine

З

звать to call (name)
зверь *m* animal
здесь here
здра́вствуйте [здраствуйте] Hello (polite)
   здравствуй [здраствуй] Hello (infomal)
зе́бра zebra
зелёный green
змея́ snake
знак sign
знако́мьтесь *refl* Please get acquainted
зо́на zone
зоопа́рк zoo

И

и and
извини́те excuse me
и́ли or
и́мя first name
и́ндекс zip code
инжене́р engineer
интере́сный *adj* interesting
интерне́т Internet
информа́ция information
Испа́ния Spain
Ита́лия Italy
их their, them

К

как how
кака́о cocoa
како́го [какова] цве́та what color
како́й *adj* what, which, what kind
Калифо́рния California
калькуля́тор calculator
Кана́да Canada
кана́л channel
капита́н captain
карата́ karate
кафе́ café
ке́мпинг campsite
кио́ск kiosk
класс classroom, class
клие́нт client
клуб club
кни́га book
код code
козёл goat
колле́га colleague
ко́лледж college
кома́нда team, command
компа́ния company
компози́тор composer
компью́тер computer
кондиционе́р air conditioner

контро́ль *m* control
конце́рт concert
конь *m* horse
коридо́р bullfight, corridor
кори́чневый brown
корри́да corrida
ко́смос cosmos, (outer) space
костю́м suit, costume
кот cat
ко́фе *m* coffee
краси́вый *adj* beautiful
кра́сный red
кре́сло armchair
крокоди́л crocodile
кто who

Л

ла́мпа lamp
лев lion
ли́лия lily
лимо́н lemon
лимона́д lemonade
литерату́ра literature
литр liter
лук onion
люк manhole

М

майоне́з mayonnaise
ма́ленький small, little
ма́льчик little boy
ма́ма mom
мандари́н tangerine
маникю́р manicure
ма́ска mask
матема́тика math
мать mother
ма́фия mafia
маши́на car, machine
меда́ль *f* medal
Ме́ксика Mexico

ме́неджер manager
меню́ menu
мета́лл metal
метро́ metro
мёд honey
микроско́п microscope
мини́стр minister
ми́нус minus
мину́та minute
мира́ж mirage
мой my
молоко́ milk
моме́нт moment
мо́ре sea
Москва́ Moscow
мост bgridge
мотоци́кл motorcycle
муж husband
музе́й museum
му́зыка music
мы we
мы́ло soap
мышь mouse
мю́сли muesli
мяч ball

Н

наря́д outfit
нас us
не not
нет no
неудо́бный uncomfortable
но́вый new
ноль *m* zero
но́мер number
нос nose
но́та note
ночь *f* night
Нью Дже́рси New Jersey
Нью Йорк New York
нюа́нс nuance
ня́ня nanny

О

образе́ц example
объём volume
огуре́ц cucumber
оди́н one
оди́ннадцать eleven
о́зеро lake
окно́ window
он he
она́ she
оно́ it, a neuter object
они́ they
о́пера opera
орке́стр orchestra
отве́т answer
Отвеча́йте! *v* Answer!
оте́ц father
отли́чно *adv* perfect, excellent
о́фис office
о́чень *adv* very
очки́ glasses, spectacles
оши́бка mistake

П

панора́ма panorama
панте́ра panther
па́па dad
па́пка folder
парк park
парла́мент parliament
партнёр partner
пассажи́р passenger
па́спорт passport
пацие́нт [пациэнт] patient
пеницили́н penicillin
пило́т pilot
пи́цца pizza
план plan
платфо́рма platform
пла́тье dress
плюс plus

Повторя́йте! *v* Repeat!

Поговори́м! *v* Let's talk!

по́езд train

пожа́луйста [пажалуста] welcome, please

пока́ bye

пока́зывать to show

поли́тика politics

понима́ть to understand

поня́тно! *adv* I see! It's clear!

попуга́й parrot

посчита́ем [пащитаем] let's count; let's calculate

президе́нт president

приве́т Hi! (informal)

при́нтер printer

пробле́ма problem

программи́ст programmer

прое́кт project

прости́те I am sorry

профе́ссия profession

пу́дель *m* poodle

пуши́стый fluffy

пчела́ bee

пюре́ puree

пятна́дцать fifteen

пять five

Р

ра́дио radio

расписа́ние schedule

ребёнок child

ре́гби rugby

рестора́н restaurant

реце́пт recipe

рис rice

риск risk

ро́бот robot

ро́за rose

ро́зовый pink

Росси́я Russia

рубль *m* ruble

ру́сский *adj* Russian

ру́чка pen

ры́ба fish

ряд row

С

саксофо́н saxophone

сала́т salad

сантиме́тр centimeter

сви́тер sweater

секрета́рь secretary (male)

секрета́рша secretary (female)

семна́дцать seventeen

семья́ family

се́рый gray

серьёзный serious, important

сестра́ sister

сигна́л signal

си́ний blue

систе́ма system

ско́лько how much, how many

сле́ва *adv* on the left

слова́рь *m* dictionary

Слу́шайте! *v* Listen!

слон elephant

снег snow

снежи́нка snowflake

соба́ка dog

сок juice

со́лнце sun

со́ус sauce

спаси́бо thank you

спорт sport

спортсме́н sportsman, athlete

спра́ва on the right

спу́тник sputnik

стадио́н stadium

стака́н glass

ста́рший older, elder

стол table

стоп *n* stop

студе́нт student (college or university)

студе́нтка student (female)

стул chair
сувени́р souvenir
суп soup
сын son
сыр cheese

Т

там there
такси́ taxi
теа́тр theater
текст text
телеви́зор TV set
телефо́н phone
те́ннис tennis
тепе́рь *adv* now, nowadays
тётя aunt
тигр tiger
то that
то́же also
торт cake
трамва́й tram
тра́нспорт transport
три three
трина́дцать thirteen
тролле́йбус trolleybus
туале́т toilet, restroom
тури́ст tourist
ты you (informal singular)

У

у́мный smart
университе́т university
упражне́ние exercise
уро́к lesson
учи́тель *m* teacher (elementary, high school)
учени́к student (male)
учени́ца student (female)
учи́тельница teacher (female)
учи́тель teacher (male)

Ф

факс fax
фи́зика physics
фильм film
фи́рма firm
фо́то photo
фотоаппара́т camera
фотогра́фия photograph
фра́за phrase
Фра́нция France
футбо́л soccer

Х

хлеб bread
хокке́й hockey
хо́лодно *adv* cold
холо́дный *adj* cold
хоро́ший *adj* good
хорошо́ *adv* good, OK, well

Ц

цвет color
цвето́к flower
цветы́ flowers
центр center

Ч

чай *n* tea
часы́ *pl* clock, watch
ча́шка cup
чек *n* check
челове́к person
чемпио́н champion
четы́ре four
четы́рнадцать fourteen
чёрный black
что [што] what, that

Ш

шестна́дцать sixteen
шесть six
шик *n* chic
широ́кий wide
шко́ла school
шко́льник schoolboy
шко́льница schoolgirl
шокола́д chocolate

Щ

щено́к puppy

Э

эконо́мика economy
э́то this

Ю

юри́ст lawyer

Я

я I
я́блоко *n* apple
язы́к language, tongue

English-Russian Dictionary

A

actor **актёр**
actress **актри́са**
address *n* **а́дрес**
administration **администра́ция**
Africa **А́фрика**
airport **аэропо́рт**
alphabet **алфави́т**
also **то́же**
America **Аме́рика**
and **а, и**
anecdote **анекдо́т**
animal **зверь**
answer *n* **отве́т**
Answer! *v* **Отвеча́йте!**
apple *n* **я́блоко**
apricot **абрико́с**
aquarium **аква́риум**
athlete **спортсме́н**
aunt **тётя**
avocado **авока́до**

B

badminton **бадминто́н**
baggage **бага́ж**
balcony **балко́н**
ball **мяч**
ballerina **балери́на**
ballet **балет**
banana **бана́н**
bank **банк**
basketball **баскетбо́л**
bear *m* **медве́дь**

beautiful **краси́вый**
bee **пчела́**
beetle **жук**
beet (beetroot) soup **борщ**
beige **бе́жевый**
belongings **вещь**
big **большо́й**
black **чёрный**
block **блок**
blue **си́ний**
   sky blue **голубо́й**
book **кни́га**
boss **босс**
botany **бота́ника**
boxing **бокс**
boy **ма́льчик** (little)
bracelet **браслет**
bridge **мост**
brother **брат**
brown **кори́чневый**
bus **авто́бус**
business **де́ло**
businessman **бизнесме́н**
bye **пока́** (informal)

C

café **кафе́**
cake **торт**
calculate *v* **счита́ть** [щитать]
calculator **калькуля́тор**
California **Калифо́рния**
camera **фотоаппара́т**
campsite **ке́мпинг**

Canada **Кана́да**
captain **капита́н**
car **маши́на**
cassette **кассе́та**
cat **кот**
center *n* **центр**
centimeter **сантиме́тр**
chair **стул**
champion **чемпио́н**
channel **кана́л**
chapter **глава́**
child **ребёнок**
check *n* **чек**
cheerful **весёлый**
cheese **сыр**
chemistry **хи́мия**
chocolate *n* **шокола́д**
chocolate *adj* **шокола́дный**
class **класс**
classroom **класс**
clear *adv* **поня́тно**
client **клие́нт**
clock *pl* **часы́**
club **клуб**
cocoa **кака́о**
code **код**
coffee *m* **ко́фе**
cold *adj* **холо́дный**
cold *adv* **хо́лодно**
colleague **колле́га**
college **ко́лледж**
color **цвет**
command **кома́нда**
comfortable **удо́бный**
company **компа́ния**
composer **компози́тор**
computer **компью́тер**
comrade **това́рищ**
concert **конце́рт**
conditioner **кондиционе́р**
control *m* **контро́ль**
cool *adj* **кла́ссный** (good)
corridor **коридо́р**

cosmos **ко́смос**
costume **костю́м, наря́д**
couch **дива́н**
country **страна́**
crocodile **крокоди́л**
crystal *adj* **хруста́льный**
cucumber **огуре́ц**
cup **ча́шка**

D

dad **па́па**
daughter **дочь**
day *m* **день**
dear **дорого́й**
designer **диза́йнер**
device **маши́на**
dialogue **диало́г**
dictionary *m* **слова́рь**
difficult *adj* **тру́дный**
diploma **дипло́м**
director **дире́ктор**
discotheque **дискоте́ка**
disk **диск**
doctor **врач**
document **докуме́нт**
dog **соба́ка**
dollar **до́ллар**
door *f* **дверь**

E

economy **эконо́мика**
eight **во́семь**
eighteen **восемна́дцать**
elder **ста́рший**
electronic **электро́нный**
elephant **слон**
eleven **оди́ннадцать**
engineer **инжене́р**
England **А́нглия**
English *adj* **англи́йский**
entrance (for vehicles) **въезд**

eternal **ве́чный**
European *n* **европе́ец** (male)
example **образе́ц**
excellent *adv* **отли́чно**
excuse me **извини́те**
exercise **упражне́ние**
expensive **дорого́й**

F

family **семья́**
far *adv* **далеко́**
father **оте́ц**
favorite **люби́мый**
fax **факс**
fifteen **пятна́дцать**
film **фильм**
firm **фи́рма**
first name **и́мя**
fir tree **ёлка**
fish **ры́ба**
five **пять**
flower **цвето́к**
flowers *pl* **цветы́**
fluffy *adj* **пуши́стый**
four **четы́ре**
fourteen **четы́рнадцать**
France **Фра́нция**
friend **друг, това́рищ**
friend (female) **подру́га**
fruit **фрукт**

G

garage **гара́ж**
gallery **галере́я**
geography **геогра́фия**
geologist **гео́лог**
Germany **Герма́ния**
giraffe **жира́ф**
girl **де́вочка** (little)
glass **стака́н**
glasses **очки́** (spectacles)

goat **козёл**
good *adj* **хоро́ший**
good *adv* **хорошо́**
gram **грамм**
grandfather **де́душка**
grandmother **ба́бушка**
green **зелёный**
gray **се́рый**
group **гру́ппа**
guest *m* **гость**
gymnastics **гимна́стика**

H

he **он**
hedgehog **ёж**
Hello! **Здра́вствуйте!** [здраствуйте] (polite);
    Здра́вствуй! [здраствуй] **приве́т!** (informal)
her **её**
hero **геро́й**
here **здесь, вот, вот здесь**
Hi! (informal) **приве́т**
hippopotamus **бегемо́т**
his **его́** [ево]
hockey **хокке́й**
home *n* **дом**
honey **мёд**
horse *m* **конь**
house **дом, зда́ние**
how **как**
how much, how many **ско́лько**
huge *adj* **огро́мный**
human being **челове́к**
husband **муж**

I

I **я**
information **информа́ция**
Internet **интерне́т**
interesting *adj* **интере́сный**
it (neuter object) **оно́**

Italy **Ита́лия**

J

jeans **джи́нсы**
juice **сок**

K

karate **карата́**
kind **до́брый**
kiosk **кио́ск**

L

lake **о́зеро**
lamp **ла́мпа, торшер** (floor lamp)
language **язы́к**
left *adv* **сле́ва** (on the left)
lemon **лимо́н**
lemonade **лимона́д**
lesson **уро́к**
letter **письмо́**
Let's talk! **Поговори́м!**
library **библиоте́ка**
light *adj* **све́тлый**
lily **ли́лия**
lion **лев**
Listen! *v* **Слу́шайте!**
liter **литр**
literature **литерату́ра**
little *adj* **ма́ленький**
a little bit *adv* **немно́жко**

M

mafia **ма́фия**
magazine **журна́л**
man **мужчи́на** [мущина]
manager **ме́неджер**
manhole **люк**
manicure **маникю́р**

mask **ма́ска**
massage **масса́ж**
math **матема́тика**
medal *f* **меда́ль**
menu **меню́**
metal **мета́лл**
metro **метро́**
Mexico **Ме́ксика**
microscope **микроско́п**
milk **молоко́**
minister **мини́стр**
minus **ми́нус**
minute **мину́та**
mirage **мира́ж**
mistake **оши́бка**
mobile **моби́льный**
mom **ма́ма**
moment **моме́нт**
Moscow **Москва́**
mother **мать**
motorcycle **мотоци́кл**
mouse **мышь**
muesli **мю́сли**
museum **музе́й**
music **му́зыка**
my **мой**

N

nanny **ня́ня**
new *adj* **но́вый**
New Jersey **Нью Дже́рси**
New York **Нью Йорк**
night *f* **ночь**
nine **де́вять**
nineteen **девятна́дцать**
noisy *adj* **шу́мный**
nose **нос**
not **не**
note **но́та**
now **сейча́с** [сичас], **тепе́рь**
nuance **нюа́нс**

O

office **кабине́т, о́фис**
often *adv* **ча́сто**
Oh! **А!**
OK *adv* **ла́дно, хорошо́**
older **ста́рший**
one **оди́н**
onion **лук**
opera **о́пера**
or **и́ли**
orange *n* **апельси́н**
orchestra **орке́стр**
outfit **наря́д**
over here **вот здесь**
over there **вон там**

P

panorama **панора́ма**
panther **панте́ра**
pants **брю́ки**
paper **бума́га**
park **парк**
Parliament **парла́мент**
patient **пацие́нт** [пациэнт]
parterre **парте́р**
partner **партнёр**
passenger **пассажи́р**
passport **па́спорт**
patient **пацие́нт** [пациэнт]
pencil **каранда́ш**
penicillin **пеницили́н**
perfect *adv* **отли́чно**
person **челове́к**
pharmacy **апте́ка**
phone **телефо́н**
photo **фо́то**
photograph **фотогра́фия**
phrase **фра́за**
physics **фи́зика**
pilot *n* **пило́т**
pineapple **анана́с**

pink **ро́зовый**
pistachio *adj* **фиста́шковый**
pizza **пи́цца**
place **ме́сто**
plan **план**
platform **платфо́рма**
please **пожа́луйста** [пажалуста]
plus **плюс**
politics *sing* **поли́тика**
poodle *m* **пу́дель**
president **президе́нт**
printer **при́нтер**
problem **пробле́ма, вопро́с**
profession **профе́ссия**
professor **профе́ссор**
programmer **программи́ст**
project **прое́кт**
pullover **джéмпер**
puppy **щено́к**
puree **пюре́**

Q

quarter **че́тверть**
question *n* **вопро́с**
quickly *adv* **бы́стро**

R

radio **ра́дио**
rain *m* **дождь**
red **кра́сный**
reddish-brown **ры́жий**
Repeat! **Повторя́йте!**
restaurant **рестора́н**
restroom **туале́т**
rice **рис**
risk **риск**
right *adv* **спра́ва** (on the right)
robot **ро́бот**
rose *n* **ро́за**
rose *adj* **ро́зовый**

row **ряд**
ruble *m* **рубль**
rugby **ре́гби**
Russia **Росси́я**

S

salad **сала́т**
sauce **со́ус**
saxophone **саксофо́н**
saxophonist **саксофони́ст**
schedule **расписа́ние**
school **шко́ла**
schoolboy **шко́льник, учени́к**
schoolgirl **шко́льница, учени́ца**
sea **мо́ре**
seat **ме́сто**
secretary **секрета́рь** (male), **секрета́рша** (female)
serious **серьёзный**
seven **семь**
seventeen **семна́дцать**
she **она́**
shorts **шо́рты**
sign (symbol) *n* **знак**
signal **сигна́л**
silver *adj* **сере́бряный**
sister **сестра́**
six **шесть**
sixteen **шестна́дцать**
small *adj* **ма́ленький**
smart **у́мный**
snake **змея́**
snow *n* **снег**
snowflake **снежи́нка**
soap **мы́ло**
soccer **футбо́л**
son **сын**
soup **суп**
souvenir **сувени́р**
Spain **Испа́ния**
sport **спорт**
sputnik **спу́тник**

stadium **стадио́н**
stamp **ма́рка**
standard **станда́рт**
stop *n* **остано́вка, стоп**
street **у́лица**
student (college or university) **студе́нт** (male), **студе́нтка** (female)
stuff *pl* **вещь**
subtitle **субти́тр**
suit *n* **костю́м**
sun **со́лнце**
sweater **сви́тер**
system **систе́ма**

T

table **стол**
tangerine **мандари́н**
teach **преподава́ть**
teacher **учи́тель**
    учи́тельница (female)
team **кома́нда**
ten **де́сять**
tennis **те́ннис**
test **экза́мен**
text **текст**
thank you **спаси́бо**
that **то, что**
theater **теа́тр**
there **вон; вон там; там**
their **их**
they **они́**
thing **вещь**
thirteen **трина́дцать**
this **э́то**
three **три**
tiger **тигр**
toilet **туале́т**
tongue **язы́к**
tourist **тури́ст**
train **по́езд**
tram **трамва́й**
transport **тра́нспорт**

tree де́рево
trick трюк
trolleybus тролле́йбус
TV set телеви́зор
twenty два́дцать
twelve двена́дцать
two два

U

Ukraine Украи́на
uncle дя́дя
university университе́т

V

vase ва́за
very о́чень
volume объём

W

watch *pl* часы́
water вода́
we мы
welcome пожа́луйста [пажалуста]
well хорошо́

what како́й, что
watch *n pl* часы́
where где
wife жена́
white бе́лый
who кто
wife жена́
window окно́
word сло́во
work *n* рабо́та

Y

yellow жёлтый
yes да
yet ещё
you (polite singular/*pl)* вы

Z

zebra зе́бра
zero *m* ноль
zip code и́ндекс
zone зо́на
zoo зоопа́рк

Available Titles

Children's Series: Age 3 - 7

1. Azbuka 1: **Coloring Russian Alphabet:** Азбука- раскраска (Step 1)
2. Azbuka 2: **Playing with Russian Letters:** Занимательная азбука (Step2)
3. Azbuka 3: **Beginning with Syllables:** Мои первые слоги (Step 3)
4. Azbuka 4: **Continuing with Syllables**: Продолжаем изучать слоги (Step 4)
5. **Animal Names and Sounds**: Кто как говорит Part 1
6. **Animal Names and Sounds: Coloring Book:** Кто как говорит Part 2
7. Propisi for Preschoolers 1: **Russian Letters: Trace and Learn:** Тренируем пальчики (Step 1)

Children's Series: Age 8 - 14

1. **Workbook 1:** Reading Russian Step By Step for Children (Book & Audio)
2. **Teacher's Manual 1**: Russian Step By Step for Children
3. **Workbook 2:** Russian Step By Step for Children (Book & Audio)
4. **Teacher's Manual 2:** Russian Step By Step for Children
5. **Workbook 3:** Reading Russian Step By Step for Children (Book & Audio)
6. **Teacher's Manual 3**: Russian Step By Step for Children
7. **Workbook 4:** Reading Russian Step By Step for Children (Book & Audio)
8. **Teacher's Manual 4**: Russian Step By Step for Children
9. Russian Handwriting 1: **Propisi 1**
10. Russian Handwriting 2: **Propisi 2**
11. Russian Handwriting 3: **Propisi 3**

Adult Learner's Series:

1. **Student Book 1 Beginner:** Russian Step By Step: School Edition (Book & Audio)
2. **Teacher's Manual 1 Beginner**: Russian Step By Step: School Edition
3. **Student Book 2 Low Intermediate:** Russian Step By Step: School Edition (Book & Audio)
4. **Teacher's Manual 2 Low Intermediate**: Russian Step By Step: School Edition
5. **Student Book Intermediate 3:** Russian Step By Step: School Edition (Book & Audio)
6. **Teacher's Manual 3 Intermediate**: Russian Step By Step: School Edition
7. **Student Book 4 Upper Intermediate:** Russian Step By Step: School Edition (Book & Audio)
8. **Teacher's Manual 4 Upper Intermediate**: Russian Step By Step: School Edition
9. Russian Handwriting 1: **Propisi 1**
10. Russian Handwriting 2: **Propisi 2**
11. Russian Handwriting 3: **Propisi 3**
12. **Verbs of Motion**: Workbook 1
13. **Verbs of Motion**: Workbook 2

18554235R00056

Printed in Poland
by Amazon Fulfillment
Poland Sp. z o.o., Wrocław